Mastering Prompt Engineering for Generative AI: Unlocking the Full Potential of AI Technology

Table of Contents

- Principles of Effective Prompt Design

- Examples of Good and Bad Prompts

- Techniques for Refining Prompts

5. Advanced Prompting Techniques

- Multi-turn Prompts

- Contextual and Sequential Prompts

- Leveraging Model Outputs

6. Domain-Specific Prompt Engineering

- Creative Writing and Storytelling

- Conversational AI

- Visual and Artistic Applications

- Scientific and Technical Domains

7. Ethics and Bias in Prompt Engineering

- Recognizing and Mitigating Bias

- Ethical Considerations

- Responsible AI Use

8. Tools and Platforms for Prompt Engineering

- Overview of Popular Tools (e.g., OpenAI Playground, AI21 Studio)
- Integrating Prompts with APIs
- Customizing and Extending Models

9. Testing and Evaluation

- Metrics for Assessing Prompt Performance
- User Feedback and Iterative Improvement
- A/B Testing and Comparative Analysis

10. Case Studies

- Real-world Examples of Successful Prompt Engineering
- Lessons Learned from Industry Applications

11. Future Trends in Generative AI and Prompt Engineering

- Emerging Technologies and Innovations

- Predictions for the Future of AI and Prompting

- Preparing for Future Developments

Introduction to Generative AI

What is Generative AI?

Generative AI refers to a class of artificial intelligence models that are designed to create new content. Unlike traditional AI models that focus on analyzing and classifying existing data, generative AI models can produce original data that mimics human creation. This can include text, images, music, and even entire virtual environments. The core idea is to generate new outputs based on the patterns and structures learned from a vast amount of training data.

At its essence, generative AI operates by predicting the next element in a sequence based on the context provided by previous elements. For example, in text generation, it predicts the next word or sentence, while in image generation, it might predict the next pixel or segment of the image. The capability to generate content that is often indistinguishable from human-created content makes generative AI a powerful and versatile tool in various fields.

History and Evolution

The journey of generative AI is marked by significant milestones and technological advancements:

1. **Early Concepts and Foundations**: The concept of generative models dates back to early AI research in the mid-20th century. Initial models, such as Markov chains and basic neural networks, laid the groundwork for more complex algorithms.

2. **Introduction of Neural Networks**: The advent of neural networks in the 1980s and 1990s brought a significant leap in AI capabilities. Models like Hopfield networks and Boltzmann machines were some of the early attempts to create generative systems.

3. **Deep Learning Revolution**: The 2000s saw the rise of deep learning, which revolutionized AI with more powerful models like Convolutional Neural Networks (CNNs) and Recurrent Neural Networks (RNNs). These models improved the ability to generate complex data, such as high-resolution images and coherent text sequences.

4. **Generative Adversarial Networks (GANs)**: In 2014, Ian Goodfellow and his colleagues introduced GANs, which consist of two neural networks—the generator and the discriminator—competing against each other. GANs marked a breakthrough in generating realistic images, videos, and other types of data.

5. **Transformer Models**: The introduction of transformer architectures, particularly the development of the Transformer model by Vaswani et al. in 2017, led to a new era in generative AI. Transformers enabled better handling of sequential data and long-range dependencies, which is crucial for tasks like text generation.

6. **Large Language Models**: The release of models like OpenAI's GPT (Generative Pre-trained Transformer) series brought generative AI to the mainstream. These models, especially GPT-3 and later versions, demonstrated unprecedented capabilities in generating human-like text, powering applications from chatbots to content creation tools.

Key Applications and Use Cases

Generative AI has a wide range of applications across various domains:

1. **Natural Language Processing (NLP)**:
   - **Text Generation**: Creating articles, stories, and poetry.
   - **Conversational Agents**: Developing chatbots and virtual assistants that can engage in human-like conversations.

- **Translation**: Improving machine translation systems.

2. **Image and Video Generation**:

   - **Art and Design**: Generating artwork, graphic designs, and animations.

   - **Deepfakes**: Creating realistic video and audio content for entertainment and media.

   - **Image Enhancement**: Improving the quality of images, such as upscaling resolution and removing noise.

3. **Music and Audio**:

   - **Composition**: Generating original music and soundtracks.

   - **Voice Synthesis**: Creating realistic human speech for virtual assistants and audiobooks.

4. **Game Development**:

- **Procedural Content Generation**: Creating dynamic game environments, characters, and storylines.

- **NPC Behavior**: Designing non-player characters with realistic interactions.

5. **Healthcare**:

   - **Drug Discovery**: Generating molecular structures for new pharmaceuticals.

   - **Medical Imaging**: Enhancing and generating medical images for diagnosis and research.

6. **Marketing and Advertising**:

   - **Personalized Content**: Creating customized marketing materials tailored to individual preferences.

   - **Ad Copywriting**: Automating the generation of persuasive advertising copy.

7. **Education and Training**:

- **Tutoring Systems**: Developing intelligent tutoring systems that provide personalized learning experiences.

- **Content Creation**: Generating educational materials and interactive content.

Generative AI continues to evolve, unlocking new possibilities and transforming various industries by

enhancing creativity, efficiency, and innovation. Its potential is vast, and as the technology advances, we can expect even more groundbreaking applications to emerge, reshaping the way we interact with and benefit from artificial intelligence.

Chapter 2: Fundamentals of Prompt Engineering

Definition and Importance

Prompt engineering is the process of designing and refining input prompts that guide generative AI models to produce desired outputs. This involves carefully crafting the text, context, and instructions given to the AI to achieve specific goals, whether it's generating creative content, answering questions, or performing complex tasks. The importance of prompt engineering lies in its direct impact on the quality, relevance, and accuracy of the AI-generated content. Effective prompt engineering ensures that the AI understands the user's intent and produces outputs that are both useful and appropriate for the given application.

Types of Prompts

Prompts can be categorized based on their structure and purpose. Understanding these types helps in selecting the most suitable prompt for a given task:

1. **Descriptive Prompts**:

   - Provide detailed instructions or descriptions to guide the AI model.

   - Example: "Write a detailed description of a sunset over the ocean."

2. **Contextual Prompts**:

   - Offer context or background information to enhance the relevance of the AI's response.

   - Example: "Given that the protagonist is a detective, write the opening scene of the story."

3. **Sequential Prompts**:

- Use a series of prompts to build a coherent and structured output over multiple turns.

  - Example: "First, describe the setting of the story. Then, introduce the main character. Finally, start the plot with an unexpected event."

4. **Question-based Prompts**:

  - Pose questions to the AI to elicit specific information or responses.

  - Example: "What are the key benefits of renewable energy sources?"

5. **Instructional Prompts**:

  - Provide explicit instructions for the AI to follow.

  - Example: "List five tips for improving mental health."

Common Challenges and Pitfalls

Despite its potential, prompt engineering comes with several challenges:

1. **Ambiguity**:

   - Vague or unclear prompts can lead to irrelevant or inaccurate outputs. It is essential to use precise language to avoid misunderstandings.

2. **Bias**:

   - Prompts can unintentionally introduce bias, reflecting or amplifying prejudices present in the training data. This can affect the fairness and neutrality of the AI's responses.

3. **Overfitting**:

   - Relying too heavily on specific phrases or examples can limit the model's creativity and versatility, leading to repetitive or predictable outputs.

4. **Complexity**:

   - Crafting effective prompts can be complex, requiring an understanding of both the AI model's capabilities and the nuances of the task at hand.

5. **Iterative Nature**:

   - Prompt engineering often requires multiple iterations to refine prompts for optimal performance, which can be time-consuming.

Chapter 3: Understanding AI Models

Overview of Generative Models

Generative AI encompasses various models, each designed to create different types of content. The most prominent generative models include:

1. **GPT (Generative Pre-trained Transformer)**:

   - Primarily used for text generation, GPT models are pre-trained on large datasets and can produce human-like text based on input prompts. They excel in tasks such as writing essays, generating code, and creating dialogue.

2. **DALL-E**:

   - Specialized in generating images from textual descriptions, DALL-E can create novel visual content that matches the given description. It is used in fields like digital art, graphic design, and creative content generation.

3. **Stable Diffusion**:

   - Focuses on generating high-quality images through advanced diffusion processes. It can produce detailed and realistic visuals, making it suitable for applications in photography, video game design, and advertising.

Model Architecture and Training

Generative AI models are built on complex neural network architectures and trained on vast datasets to learn patterns and structures. The training process involves several key steps:

1. **Data Collection**:

   - Large datasets are gathered from diverse sources to provide a comprehensive training ground for the AI model. This data includes text, images, and other forms of content.

2. **Pre-training**:

  - During pre-training, the model learns general language patterns and knowledge from the collected data. This phase equips the model with a broad understanding of language and context.

3. **Fine-tuning**:

  - Fine-tuning involves training the model on specific tasks or datasets to enhance its performance in particular applications. This step customizes the model to better handle targeted tasks.

4. **Evaluation**:

  - The model's performance is evaluated using various metrics to ensure it meets the desired standards. This involves testing the model on unseen data and adjusting parameters as needed.

Strengths and Limitations

Strengths:

- **Versatility**: Generative AI models can handle a wide range of tasks, from text generation to image creation, making them highly versatile tools.

- **Creativity**: These models can produce creative and novel outputs, often surpassing human capabilities in generating unique content.

- **Efficiency**: AI models can generate content quickly and at scale, significantly reducing the time and effort required for manual creation.

Limitations:

- **Bias**: AI models can reflect and amplify biases present in their training data, leading to unfair or prejudiced outputs.

- **Resource Intensive**: Training and running generative AI models require substantial computational resources and energy, which can be a barrier to accessibility.

- **Quality Dependence**: The quality of the generated content heavily depends on the quality and diversity of the training data. Poor training data can result in low-quality outputs.

- **Complexity**: Understanding and effectively using these models requires significant expertise in AI and machine learning.

This detailed overview of prompt engineering and AI models provides a foundational understanding of the principles, challenges, and techniques involved in guiding generative AI to produce high-quality outputs.

Chapter 4: Crafting Effective Prompts

Principles of Effective Prompt Design

Clarity: Ensure that prompts are clear and easy to understand. Use straightforward language and avoid ambiguity to guide the AI model accurately.

Relevance: Make sure that prompts are directly related to the desired output. Provide context or instructions that align with the task at hand to help the AI generate appropriate content.

Conciseness: Keep prompts concise and to the point. Avoid unnecessary complexity or verbosity that could confuse the AI model and lead to irrelevant outputs.

Examples of Good and Bad Prompts

Good Prompt: "Write a short story about a character who discovers a hidden treasure in an abandoned house."

Why it's good: This prompt provides a clear task (writing a short story) and includes specific details (discovering a hidden treasure in an abandoned house) to guide the AI model towards generating relevant content.

Bad Prompt: "Story about finding something."

Why it's bad: This prompt is too vague and lacks specific details. It does not provide enough guidance for the AI model to generate a coherent narrative.

Techniques for Refining Prompts

Iterative Testing: Continuously test and adjust prompts based on the AI model's outputs. Pay attention to the quality and relevance of the generated content and make refinements as needed.

Feedback Incorporation: Gather feedback from users or stakeholders on the effectiveness of prompts. Use this feedback to identify areas for improvement and make adjustments to enhance prompt quality.

Specificity Enhancement: Add more specific details or instructions to prompts to narrow down the AI model's focus and improve the relevance of generated content. Clarify any ambiguities and provide additional context where necessary.

By following these principles and techniques, you can craft effective prompts that guide AI models to produce high-quality and relevant outputs for a variety of tasks and applications.

Chapter 5: Advanced Prompting Techniques

Multi-turn Prompts

Multi-turn prompts involve a series of interconnected prompts and responses to build a coherent and complex output. This technique is particularly useful in conversational AI and storytelling, where the context evolves over multiple interactions. Each prompt builds on the previous one, creating a more dynamic and engaging interaction with the AI model.

Example in Conversational AI:

1. **User**: "Tell me about the weather today."

2. **AI**: "It's sunny and warm, with temperatures around 75°F. Would you like to know about any specific activities for today?"

3. **User**: "Yes, what outdoor activities are good for sunny weather?"

4. **AI**: "You can go for a hike, have a picnic, or visit a local park. Do you need recommendations for any specific locations?"

This sequence allows the AI to maintain context and provide more relevant and tailored responses.

Contextual and Sequential Prompts

Contextual Prompts provide background information or previous interactions to inform the AI's response. This technique helps the AI understand the broader context, leading to more accurate and relevant outputs.

Example:

- **Contextual Prompt**: "In our last conversation, we discussed the benefits of renewable energy. Can you explain the advantages of solar power specifically?"

Sequential Prompts involve guiding the AI through a step-by-step process, ensuring that the generated content is structured and logical. This method is useful for tasks that require a clear progression or detailed explanation.

Example:

1. **Sequential Prompt**: "First, describe the basic principles of solar power. Then, explain how solar panels convert sunlight into electricity. Finally, discuss the environmental benefits of using solar energy."

Leveraging Model Outputs

Leveraging model outputs involves using the AI's previous responses as new inputs to refine and expand on the content.

This iterative approach allows for more sophisticated and detailed results.

Example in Creative Writing:

1. **Initial Prompt**: "Write an introduction for a mystery novel set in a small town."

2. **AI Output**: "In the quaint town of Hollow Creek, the air always seemed thick with secrets. On a foggy evening, a shadowy figure slipped into the old library..."

3. **Follow-up Prompt**: "Continue the story by describing the mysterious figure and their purpose in the library."

This method builds on the AI's initial output, adding depth and complexity to the narrative.

Chapter 6: Domain-Specific Prompt Engineering

Creative Writing and Storytelling

In creative writing and storytelling, prompts can be designed to generate compelling narratives, character dialogues, and plot twists. The key is to provide clear and vivid descriptions that inspire the AI to produce imaginative and engaging content.

Example:

- **Prompt**: "Write a short story about a detective who discovers a hidden room in an old mansion, leading to a series of unexpected events."

Conversational AI

For conversational AI, prompts need to be crafted to guide chatbots and virtual assistants in providing accurate and engaging responses. This involves anticipating user needs and creating prompts that elicit informative and helpful answers.

Example:

- **Prompt**: "You are a virtual assistant for a travel website. A user asks for recommendations on family-friendly activities in Paris. Provide a detailed response."

Visual and Artistic Applications

In visual and artistic applications, prompts can guide AI models to create unique artworks, graphic designs, and animations. The prompts should be descriptive and specific to achieve the desired visual output.

Example:

- **Prompt**: "Create an abstract painting inspired by the colors and movement of a sunrise over the ocean."

Scientific and Technical Domains

In scientific and technical domains, prompts can be used to generate technical documents, research summaries, and complex data visualizations. These prompts should be precise and informative to ensure the AI produces accurate and relevant content.

Example:

- **Prompt**: "Write a summary of the latest research on quantum computing, highlighting the key findings and potential applications."

Chapter 7: Ethics and Bias in Prompt Engineering

Recognizing and Mitigating Bias

Recognizing and mitigating bias in AI-generated content is crucial to ensure fairness and accuracy. This involves identifying potential biases in the training data and prompts, and implementing strategies to minimize their impact.

Example:

- **Strategy**: Use diverse and representative training data to reduce biases and regularly review and update prompts to avoid reinforcing stereotypes.

Ethical Considerations

Ethical considerations in prompt engineering involve ensuring that the use of generative AI aligns with ethical guidelines, including transparency, accountability, and respect for user privacy.

Example:

- **Guideline**: Clearly disclose when users are interacting with an AI and ensure that their data is protected and used responsibly.

Responsible AI Use

Responsible AI use promotes fair and ethical applications of AI technologies, avoiding harmful or malicious uses. This includes setting clear guidelines for acceptable uses of AI and monitoring outputs for compliance with ethical standards.

Example:

- **Policy**: Implement policies that prevent the use of AI for generating harmful content, such as misinformation, deepfakes, or discriminatory material.

These detailed sections provide a comprehensive understanding of advanced prompting techniques, domain-specific applications, and the ethical considerations necessary for responsible and effective prompt engineering.

Chapter 7: Ethics and Bias in Prompt Engineering

Recognizing and Mitigating Bias

Bias in AI can lead to unfair or inaccurate outputs, reflecting or amplifying prejudices present in the training data. Recognizing and mitigating bias involves several steps:

1. **Identify Potential Biases**:

- Examine the training data for imbalances or stereotypes. Biases can be related to race, gender, age, socioeconomic status, and more.

- Analyze model outputs to spot recurring patterns of bias.

2. **Mitigation Strategies**:

- **Diverse Training Data**: Ensure the training dataset is diverse and representative of different groups and perspectives.

- **Bias Detection Tools**: Use tools specifically designed to detect and measure bias in AI models.

- **Prompt Review**: Regularly review and update prompts to avoid reinforcing existing biases.

Example:

- **Bias Detection Tool**: Implementing tools like AI Fairness 360 (AIF360) to identify and mitigate biases in AI models.

Ethical Considerations

Ethical considerations in prompt engineering focus on the responsible use of AI and ensuring that AI applications align with moral and societal values:

1. **Transparency**:

   - Clearly disclose when users are interacting with AI-generated content.

   - Explain how AI models are trained and how they work.

2. **Accountability**:

   - Establish clear lines of responsibility for the development and deployment of AI models.

   - Implement mechanisms for users to report issues or concerns with AI outputs.

3. **Privacy**:

- Ensure that user data is protected and used responsibly.

- Obtain explicit consent from users before collecting and using their data.

Example:

- **Transparency Practice**: Informing users that they are interacting with a chatbot and explaining its purpose and limitations.

Responsible AI Use

Promoting responsible AI use involves setting guidelines and policies to prevent harmful applications of AI:

1. **Guidelines for Use**:

   - Develop and enforce guidelines that outline acceptable uses of AI technology.

- Prohibit the use of AI for generating harmful content, such as deepfakes, misinformation, or discriminatory material.

2. **Monitoring and Compliance**:

   - Regularly monitor AI outputs to ensure compliance with ethical guidelines.

   - Implement corrective actions if the AI produces harmful or biased content.

Example:

- **Prohibited Use Policy**: Creating policies that prevent the use of AI for generating hate speech or false information.

Chapter 8: Tools and Platforms for Prompt Engineering

Overview of Popular Tools

Several tools and platforms facilitate prompt engineering by providing user-friendly interfaces and powerful functionalities:

1. **OpenAI Playground**:

   - A web-based tool that allows users to interact with OpenAI's models, test prompts, and see immediate outputs.

   - Features include adjustable parameters and the ability to save and share prompts.

2. **AI21 Studio**:

   - Offers a platform for experimenting with AI21's language models.

- Provides features for customizing prompts and integrating AI models into applications.

3. **Other Tools**:

   - **Hugging Face**: Provides a wide range of pre-trained models and a platform for experimenting with prompts.

   - **Google AI**: Offers tools for AI research and application development.

Integrating Prompts with APIs

Integrating prompts with APIs allows for scalable and automated use of AI models in various applications:

1. **API Integration**:

   - Use APIs to send prompts to AI models and receive generated outputs programmatically.

- Examples include OpenAI's API, which provides endpoints for text generation, summarization, and more.

2. **Automation**:

  - Automate tasks such as content creation, customer support, and data analysis by integrating AI models into existing workflows.

Example:

- **API Integration**: Using OpenAI's API to generate automated customer support responses based on user queries.

Customizing and Extending Models

Customizing and extending AI models can enhance their performance for specific tasks or domains:

1. **Fine-tuning**:

  - Fine-tune pre-trained models on specific datasets to improve their relevance and accuracy for targeted applications.

  - Example: Fine-tuning a language model on legal documents to improve its performance in legal text generation.

2. **Custom Models**:

  - Develop custom models tailored to specific needs by adjusting parameters and incorporating additional training data.

Example:

- **Custom Model**: Creating a custom model for generating medical research summaries by fine-tuning on medical literature.

Chapter 9: Testing and Evaluation

Metrics for Assessing Prompt Performance

Evaluating the performance of prompts involves using both quantitative and qualitative metrics:

1. **Quantitative Metrics**:

   - **Accuracy**: Measures how correctly the AI's outputs match the expected results.

   - **Coherence**: Evaluates the logical consistency of the generated content.

2. **Qualitative Metrics**:

   - **Relevance**: Assesses how well the AI's outputs align with the user's intent.

   - **Creativity**: Measures the originality and inventiveness of the generated content.

Example:

- **Coherence Metric**: Using perplexity to measure how well a language model predicts a sample of text.

User Feedback and Iterative Improvement

User feedback is crucial for refining prompts and improving AI performance:

1. **Feedback Collection**:

   - Gather user feedback on the relevance, accuracy, and quality of AI-generated outputs.

   - Use surveys, direct feedback mechanisms, and usage data to collect insights.

2. **Iterative Improvement**:

- Continuously refine prompts based on user feedback and performance metrics.

- Implement changes incrementally and test their impact on the AI's performance.

Example:

- **Feedback Loop**: Implementing a feedback system where users rate the helpfulness of AI-generated responses, and using this data to improve prompt design.

A/B Testing and Comparative Analysis

A/B testing involves comparing different prompts to determine which performs better:

1. **A/B Testing**:

   - Create multiple versions of a prompt and test them with different user groups.

- Analyze the results to identify which prompt version yields the best outcomes.

2. **Comparative Analysis**:

   - Compare the performance of different prompts using predefined metrics.

   - Use statistical methods to determine the significance of the differences in performance.

Example:

- **A/B Testing**: Testing two versions of a customer service prompt to see which one results in higher user satisfaction.

Chapter 10: Case Studies

Real-world Examples of Successful Prompt Engineering

Examining real-world examples can provide valuable insights into effective prompt engineering practices:

1. **Example 1**: A financial services company using prompt engineering to generate detailed investment reports, improving efficiency and accuracy.

2. **Example 2**: An e-commerce platform enhancing customer interaction through conversational AI, resulting in increased customer satisfaction and sales.

Lessons Learned from Industry Applications

Analyzing industry applications helps identify best practices and common challenges:

1. **Best Practices**:

   - Start with clear and specific prompts.

   - Continuously refine and test prompts based on feedback and performance data.

   - Ensure ethical guidelines are followed to avoid biases and harmful outputs.

2. **Common Challenges**:

   - Balancing prompt specificity with flexibility.

   - Mitigating biases in AI-generated content.

   - Ensuring user privacy and data security.

Example:

- **Lesson Learned**: A technology company discovering that iterative testing and user feedback significantly improved the accuracy and relevance of their AI-generated content.

Chapter 11: Future Trends in Generative AI and Prompt Engineering

Emerging Technologies and Innovations

Staying informed about emerging technologies and innovations in generative AI is crucial:

1. **New Models and Architectures**:

   - Development of more advanced and efficient AI models.

   - Innovations in model architectures, such as transformers and diffusion models.

2. **Integration with Other Technologies**:

   - Combining generative AI with augmented reality (AR), virtual reality (VR), and other emerging technologies to create immersive experiences.

Example:

- **Emerging Technology**: The rise of multimodal AI models that can handle both text and image generation.

Predictions for the Future of AI and Prompting

Predictions for the future of AI and prompting include:

1. **Increased Personalization**:

   - AI models will become more adept at personalizing content based on individual user preferences and behaviors.

2. **Enhanced Creativity**:

   - Advances in AI will lead to more creative and sophisticated outputs, pushing the boundaries of what generative models can achieve.

Example:

- **Future Prediction**: AI models capable of generating complex, interactive narratives in real-time, revolutionizing the entertainment industry.

Preparing for Future Developments

Preparing for future developments involves:

1. **Continuous Learning**:

   - Stay updated with the latest research and advancements in AI and prompt engineering.

   - Participate in professional development opportunities, such as workshops and courses.

2. **Adapting to Change**:

   - Be flexible and open to adopting new tools and techniques as they emerge.

- Foster a culture of innovation and experimentation within your organization.

Example:

- **Preparing for Change**: Implementing a continuous learning program to keep your team updated with the latest AI trends and technologies.

These detailed sections provide a comprehensive understanding of the ethical considerations, tools, techniques, and future trends in prompt engineering and generative AI, equipping you with the knowledge to effectively utilize and innovate in this rapidly evolving field.

www.ingramcontent.com/pod-product-compliance
Lightning Source LLC
LaVergne TN
LVHW051620050326
832903LV00033B/4584